Harold R Foster

Prince Valiant

D1430594

COMPRISING PAGES 1992 THROUGH 2035

The Mark of Cain

FANTAGRAPHICS BOOKS

ABOUT THIS EDITION:

Produced in cooperation with the Danish publisher Carlsen and several other publishers around the world, this new edition of PRINCE VALIANT is intended to be the definitive compilation of Hal Foster's masterpiece.

In addition to this volume, Fantagraphics Books has in stock 29 more collections of Foster's Valiant work (Vols. 2, 9-33, 41-44). After completing the 40-volume run of Foster's series, we are now continuing with the John Cullen Murphy drawn continuation of the strip.

ABOUT THE PUBLISHER:

FANTAGRAPHICS BOOKS has dedicated itself to bringing readers the finest in comic book and comic strip material, both new and old. Its "classics" division includes *The Complete E.C. Segar Popeye*, the *Complete Little Nemo in Slumberland* hardcover collection, and *Pogo* and *Krazy Kat* reprints. Its "modern" division is responsible for such works as *Love and Rockets* by Los Bros. Hernandez, Dave Cooper's *Weasel*, Daniel Clowes's *Eightball*, Chris Ware's *ACME*, and American editions of work by Muñoz & Sampayo, Lewis Trondheim, and F. Solano Lopez, as well as *The Complete Crumb Comics*.

PREVIOUS VOLUMES IN THIS SERIES:

PRINCE VALIANT, Volume 45
"The Mark of Cain"
comprising pages 1992 (April 13, 1975) through 2035 (February 8, 1976)
Published by Fantagraphics Books, 7563 Lake City Way NE, Seattle, WA 98115
Editorial Co-Ordinator: Henning Kure and Jens Trasborg
Cover colored by Jesper Ejsing
Cover inked by Jan Kjær Jensen
Fantagraphics Books staff: Kim Thompson and Peppy White
Copyright © 2002 King Features Syndicate, Inc., Bull's, Interpresse, & Fantagraphics Books, Inc.
Printed in Denmark   ISBN 1-56097-488-5   First Printing: Summer, 2002

Our Story: BELLA GROSSI SENDS HIS EMISSARIES BEFORE THE GATES OF THESSALRIGA DEMANDING SURRENDER ON THE CRUEL TERMS HE HAS LAID DOWN.

TO GIVE EMPHASIS TO HIS DEMANDS HE EXHIBITS WHAT IS LEFT OF THEIR KING. *"THIS IS WHAT BEFALLS ALL WHO OPPOSE MY WILL!"*

KING LEOFRIC RAISES HIS HEAD, AND IN A GREAT VOICE CRIES, *"FIGHT! FIGHT! I, YOUR KING, COMMAND YOU!"*

ODO IS SHAKEN. HE HAS NEVER EXPERIENCED SUCH CRUELTY. *"MY FATHER, MY POOR FATHER!"* HE MOANS. DUPUY REPLIES, *"IT IS YOUR DUTY TO SAVE YOUR FATHER NO MATTER WHAT THE COST. I WILL GO TO BELLA GROSSI AND TRY TO SOFTEN HIS HARSH TERMS."*

DUPUY KNEELS IN THE DUST BEFORE BELLA. *"MASTER, MY WORK IS DONE, FOR I HAVE CONVINCED PRINCE ODO TO PAY THE RANSOM AND OPEN THE GATES OF THE CITY, IF YOU RETURN KING LEOFRIC."*

"I HAVE LOWERED THE CHAIN AND LET YOUR FLEET INTO THE HARBOR. I HAVE TAKEN ALL THE WAR MACHINES FROM THE FORTRESS AND PLACED THEM WHERE THEY FELL INTO YOUR HANDS.

1992

"AS MY PORTION OF THE PLUNDER OF THESSALRIGA I CLAIM IN ADDITION... THE LADY GRANIA!"

PRINCE VALIANT HAS TRAINED A FAIR NUMBER OF WARRIORS INTO A MOUNTED TROOP. NOW HE GOES TO PRESENT HIS BATTLE PLANS TO THE COUNCIL.

NEXT WEEK-Wounded Dignity

4-13

Our Story: PRINCE VALIANT HAS TRAINED A TROOP OF MOUNTED WARRIORS WITH WHICH TO HARRY THE BESIEGERS. EAGERLY HE ENTERS THE COUNCIL CHAMBER TO OFFER HIS PLAN.

BUT PRINCE ODO HAS LISTENED TO THE TRAITOR DUPUY, AND ANNOUNCES: "MY FIRST DUTY IS TO MY FATHER, THE KING! I WILL SURRENDER THESSALRIGA TO BELLA GROSSI FOR HIS RANSOM!"

VAL DOES NOT LOSE HIS TEMPER, BUT SPEAKS CALMLY: "A KING'S DUTY IS TO THE PEOPLE HE RULES. YOUR FATHER WOULD DIE OF SHAME SHOULD YOU LET BELLA GROSSI'S CUTTHROATS INTO HIS CITY!"

THEN PRINCESS GRANIA STANDS BEFORE HIM. "I WAS SENT HERE TO BECOME YOUR BRIDE. YOU SAID YOU LOVED ME. WHAT OF ME, NOW? DO I BECOME PART OF THE PLUNDER FOR THOSE MERCILESS PIRATES?"

"GO AWAY, ALL OF YOU, I MUST THINK." HE BLUNDERS FROM THE CHAMBER AND CLIMBS TO THE TOWER. HERE, ARCHERS ARE KEEPING THE ENEMY AT A DISTANCE, AND THE ENEMY RETALIATES WITH CATAPULTS.

A HEAVY MISSILE HITS THE TOWER, ROCK FRAGMENTS FLY AND ONE HITS ODO. FOR THE FIRST TIME IN HIS LIFE. HE SUFFERS PAIN.

A GREAT CHANGE COMES OVER HIM. ANGRILY HE SNATCHES UP A DISCARDED BOW, FITS AN ARROW AND AIMS TOWARD THE ENEMY..... THE ARROW ONLY SPINS IN THE AIR AND FALLS.

1993

VAL EXAMINES THE BOW. "THE BOWSTRING IS WORN, TOO THICK TO FIT AN ARROW." FOR A MOMENT HE IS LOST IN THOUGHT. "YOUR HIGHNESS, YOU HAVE JUST SHOWN US HOW TO WIN THE WAR!"

NEXT WEEK - The Fletchers 4-20

Prince Valiant

IN THE DAYS OF KING ARTHUR

by HAL FOSTER

Our Story: PRINCE VALIANT EXAMINES THE DEFECTIVE BOWSTRING. "UNLESS THE NOCK OF THE ARROW FITS THE BOWSTRING PERFECTLY," HE EXPLAINS, "THE WEAPON IS USELESS.

"WHEN BATTLE LINES ARE FORMED, THE ARCHERS ADVANCE BEFORE THE FOOT SOLDIERS AND STRIVE BY SHEER FIREPOWER TO SOFTEN THE ENEMY RANKS. WHEN THEY HAVE SPENT THEIR OWN SUPPLY OF ARROWS, THEY RETRIEVE THE ENEMY ARROWS TO CONTINUE THE BARRAGE."

AT THE ARMORY, THE IDEA IS EXPLAINED TO THE HEAD FLETCHER. THEREAFTER, THE BUILDING HUMS WITH ACTIVITY NIGHT AND DAY.

NOW THE PEOPLE OF THESSALRIGA BEGIN TO FEEL THE PINCH OF HUNGER, WHILE THE FORTRESS BEGINS TO CRUMBLE UNDER THE BATTERING OF THE CATAPULTS.

DUPUY, THE TRAITOR, STANDS BEFORE BELLA GROSSI: "MASTER, I HAVE CONVINCED PRINCE ODO THAT HE SHOULD SURRENDER. THEY WILL ACCEPT ANY TERMS YOU OFFER, FOR THEY ARE WEAK AND HAVE SHOWN NO RESISTANCE."

BELLA GROSSI SENDS HIS EMISSARY INTO THE CITY. THEN, SURROUNDED BY HIS OFFICERS, HE STANDS BEFORE HIS ARMY TO RECEIVE THE SURRENDER OF THESSALRIGA.

ODO RECEIVES THE ULTIMATUM IN FEAR AND INDECISION. "WHAT WERE THE LAST WORDS OF YOUR GALLANT FATHER?" DEMANDS VAL.
"FIGHT," ANSWERS ODO. "AND WHAT SAY YOU?" ASKS VAL.
AT LAST HIS MANHOOD AWAKENS. "WE FIGHT!" HE SHOUTS.

BELLA GROSSI RECEIVES AN ANSWER: "NO ENEMY HAS EVER SET FOOT WITHIN THESSALRIGA, NOR WILL A FAT MUJIK AND HIS WATERFRONT RIFFRAFF!"
NEXT WEEK- *The Message of the Wild Geese*
1994   4-27

Prince Valiant
IN THE DAYS OF KING ARTHUR
BY HAL FOSTER

Our Story: BELLA GROSSI, MOST FEARED OF CORSAIRS, GOES WHITE WITH RAGE; HE HAS BEEN INSULTED BEFORE HIS WHOLE ARMY. HE MUST VENT HIS AWFUL RAGE ON SOMETHING.

SLOWLY HE TURNS TOWARD DUPUY, HIS SPY, AND DUPUY SCREAMS. HE IS LED AWAY STILL SCREAMING, FOR HE KNOWS THE FATE OF THOSE WHO FAIL BELLA GROSSI.

AT LAST THE SIGN PRINCE VALIANT HAS BEEN AWAITING. DOWN THE HIGHWAY IN THE SKY COME WAVE AFTER WAVE OF WILD GEESE. "AT LAST! A STORM IS ON THE WAY, DRIVING THE GEESE BEFORE IT. TOMORROW WE DO BATTLE!"

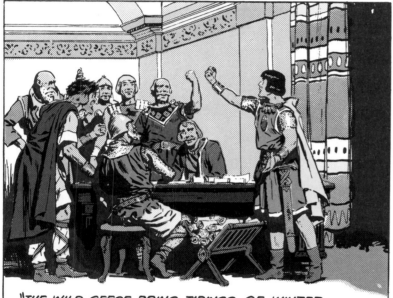

"THE WILD GEESE BRING TIDINGS OF WINTER STORMS COMING DOWN FROM THE NORTH. WE NORTHMEN ARE USED TO THE COLD, BUT OUR ENEMY COMES FROM WARMER CLIMES. THEIR HANDS WILL BE NUMB. AT DAWN WE DO BATTLE!"

IN THE DARKNESS BEFORE DAWN THE FORTRESS GATES SWING OPEN, AND THE HARDY WARRIORS OF THESSALRIGA MARCH OUT AND FORM THEIR BATTLE LINE. THE STORM FORETOLD BY THE GEESE IS BEGINNING.

TRUMPETS SOUND THE ALARM IN BELLA GROSSI'S CAMP, AND THE SHIVERING PIRATES LEAVE THE SHELTER OF THEIR TENTS AND FACE THE BITTER WIND.

1995

BELLA SNARLS WITH RAGE. TO MOVE FORWARD WOULD BRING HIS ARMY WITHIN RANGE OF ARCHERS FROM THE BATTLEMENTS. THE NORTHMEN STAND IDLY WHILE HIS MEN FREEZE.

TO THE CAPTAIN OF ARCHERS, VAL SAYS: "GO NOW INTO POSITION AND FACE THE ENEMY ARCHERS. YOU WILL SUFFER HEAVY LOSSES, BUT WHEN HE HAS EMPTIED HIS QUIVER HE WILL HAVE NO MORE ARROWS."

NEXT WEEK: The Secret Weapon 5-4

Prince Valiant IN THE DAYS OF KING ARTHUR
by HAL FOSTER

Our Story: THE BATTLE BEGINS, ARCHERS LEADING THE WAY FILLING THE AIR WITH A CLOUD OF ARROWS. QUIVERS ARE EMPTIED AND NOW EACH SIDE MUST RETRIEVE THE SPENT ARROWS OF THE ENEMY TO CONTINUE THE ASSAULT.

VAL'S STRATEGY IS A SUCCESS. THE SMALLER NOCK OF THE NORTHMEN'S ARROWS WILL NOT FIT THE THICK BOWSTRINGS OF THE CORSAIRS' BOWS. THEY ARE USELESS.

A TRUMPET SOUNDS AND THE WARRIORS OF THESSALRIGA CHARGE, SHOUTING. IN PANIC THE PIRATES FLEE TO THEIR OWN TIGHTLY PACKED LINE, AND IN THEIR STRUGGLE TO GET THROUGH TO SAFETY, HINDER THEIR COMRADES.

WHILE CONFUSION REIGNS, PRINCE VALIANT RELEASES HIS SECRET WEAPON: THE MOUNTED TROOP HE HAD BEEN TRAINING. THE THUNDER OF POUNDING HOOVES, THE GLEAMING LANCE-POINTS, IS MORE THAN THIS VICIOUS RIFFRAFF OF THE SEA CAN FACE. THE BATTLE IS WON. THE SLAUGHTER BEGINS.

BELLA GROSSI WATCHES THE TIDE OF BATTLE TURN AGAINST HIM, AND HIS DREAM OF BECOMING MASTER OF THE BALTIC FADES.

1996

ON THE BEACH HE FINDS A BOAT AND, LEAVING HIS FOLLOWERS TO THE QUESTIONABLE MERCY OF THE MEN OF THESSALRIGA, PULLS AWAY INTO THE BITTER NORTH WIND.

NEXT WEEK—*Bella Grossi's Return*

5-11

Prince Valiant
IN THE DAYS OF KING ARTHUR
by HAL FOSTER

Our Story: THESSALRIGA IS SAVED. AND THROUGH THE GRIM WRECKAGE OF WAR THEY SEARCH FOR THE BODY OF BELLA GROSSI, FOR THERE WILL BE NO SECURITY AS LONG AS HE LIVES.

WHEN FIRST THE TIDE OF BATTLE TURNED AGAINST HIM, HE ABANDONED HIS ARMY. IN A SMALL BOAT HE PULLED AWAY INTO THE GATHERING STORM. FREEZING RAIN CHANGED TO SNOW.

BELLA GROSSI RETURNS TO THESSALRIGA.

NEXT WEEK— Winter Voyage

1997

5-18

Prince Valiant
BY HAL FOSTER

Our Story: WAR DOES NOT END WITH VICTORY. THE WEARY VICTORS MUST REPAIR THE DAMAGE. THE WAR MACHINES BELLA GROSSI CONSTRUCTED MAKE A FITTING FUNERAL PYRE.

WHAT IS LEFT OF KING LEOFRIC IS RESCUED, FOR BELLA'S TORTURERS HAD LEFT IN A HURRY AND HAD NEGLECTED TO FINISH THEIR BUSINESS.

NOW THE HAPPY ENDING. PRINCE ODO HAD FOUGHT BRAVELY, WOUNDING ONLY ONE OF HIS OWN BODYGUARDS. PRINCESS GRANIA'S CONTEMPT TURNS TO ADORATION.

KING LEOFRIC IS PATCHED UP WELL ENOUGH TO ATTEND THE VICTORY FEAST. AFTER THE LONG WEEKS OF PERIL THEIR JOY IS UNRESTRAINED, AND MANY A WARRIOR WHO HAD SURVIVED ENEMY WEAPONS UNSCATHED, IS FELLED BY A FLOWING MEAD-CUP.

PRINCE VALIANT BEGINS THE LONG HOMEWARD JOURNEY. SAILING PAST DANELAND HE IS PLEASED TO SEE A FEW BURNING FARMSTEADS. FOR THIS MEANS THE DANES HAVE CEASED THEIR SEA-RAIDING AND ARE HOME TO SETTLE LOCAL DIFFERENCES.

THE NORTH SEA GREETS THEM WITH WIND AND WAVE, AGAINST WHICH NEITHER SAIL NOR OAR CAN MAKE HEADWAY.

RELUCTANTLY HE TURNS SOUTHWEST AND HEADS TOWARD BRITAIN. MANY STORM-TOSSED DAYS LATER THEY FIND THE THAMES AND LAND AT LONDINIUM.

VAL SETS OUT FOR CAMELOT. BUT NOW HE TRAVELS IN LUXURY, A SQUIRE TO TEND THE HORSES, TWO SERVANTS AND A PAVILION TO SHELTER HIM AT NIGHT.

1998   NEXT WEEK- Camelot 5-25

Our Story: PRINCE VALIANT SETS OUT FOR CAMELOT. HIS ESCORT GRUMBLES, BUT NOT HE. AFTER A MONTH SPENT IN AN OPEN BOAT EXPOSED TO A WINTRY SEA, THIS IS A RELIEF.

AT NIGHT THEY SCRAPE AWAY THE SLUSH, SET UP THE PAVILION AND BUILD A ROARING FIRE.

IN THE CENTER OF THE PAVILION THEY DIG A SHALLOW HOLE AND ROLL IN HOT ROCKS FROM THE FIREPLACE, LIGHTLY COVERING THEM WITH EARTH TO KEEP IN THE HEAT.

THEY TRAVEL LEAGUE AFTER LEAGUE OF DENSE FOREST IN RAIN AND SNOW, BUT TO VAL THIS IS A VACATION FROM HIS DANGEROUS DUTIES.

AS THE END OF THEIR JOURNEY APPROACHES, MANY KNIGHTS AND THEIR FAMILIES JOIN THEM, ALL ON THEIR WAY TO CAMELOT.

AT LAST CAMELOT IS SEEN, ALL AGLOW IN THE SUNLIGHT, A MONUMENT TO JUSTICE AND CHIVALRY THAT ILLUMINATED THE WORLD FOR, OH, SO SHORT A TIME.

6-1

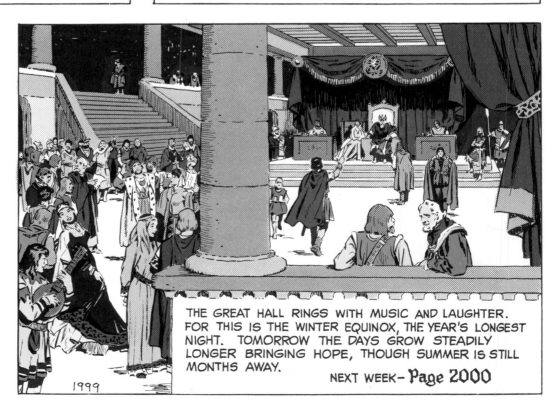

THE GREAT HALL RINGS WITH MUSIC AND LAUGHTER. FOR THIS IS THE WINTER EQUINOX, THE YEAR'S LONGEST NIGHT. TOMORROW THE DAYS GROW STEADILY LONGER BRINGING HOPE, THOUGH SUMMER IS STILL MONTHS AWAY.

NEXT WEEK - Page 2000

1999

Prince Valiant

BY HAL FOSTER

Our Story: KING AGUAR OF THULE LANDS IN BRITAIN WITH HIS QUEEN AND FIVE-YEAR-OLD SON, PRINCE VALIANT.

THE YOUNG PRINCE SPENDS HIS BOYHOOD IN THE WILD FENS LEARNING THE HUNTER'S SKILL AND THE ART OF SURVIVAL.

HE MEETS SIR GAWAIN AND A LIFELONG FRIENDSHIP BEGINS.

IN KING ARTHUR HE FINDS A LEADER WORTH SERVING TO THE VERY END. BUT IT IS GUINEVERE'S SMILE THAT INSPIRES HIM TO MASTER THE ARTS OF CHIVALRY.

THEY RIDE TO CAMELOT AND THERE HE WILL SPEND MONTHS AND YEARS IN HARD TRAINING.

THE 'SINGING SWORD' FLASHED LIKE LIGHTNING, AS HE HELD THE BRIDGE AT DUNDORN GLEN AGAINST A SAXON RAIDING PARTY UNTIL HELP ARRIVED.

AFTER THE GREAT BATTLE OF THE FENS, KING ARTHUR CALLED FOR ONE PARTICULAR HERO. DRAWING EXCALIBUR, HE TOUCHED EACH SHOULDER: "RISE, SIR VALIANT, *KNIGHT OF THE ROUND TABLE.*"

THE NEW-MADE KNIGHT SO HARASSED ATTILA THE HUN, THAT HIS CROSSING OF THE ALPS WAS DELAYED, GIVING TIME FOR ATEUS TO CONTRIVE HIS DEFEAT AT CHALONS.

SHIPWRECKED IN THE AEGEAN SEA HE BEHELD ALETA, GREY-EYED QUEEN OF THE MISTY ISLES. THROUGH SORCERY, SHE CAST A SPELL UPON HIM THAT TROUBLED HIM, BUT PLEASANTLY, FOR THE REST OF HIS LIFE.

BOLTAR, THAT HONEST MERCHANT AND PIRATE, CAME ROARING INTO HIS LIFE AND REMAINED FOREVER HIS FRIEND.

HAL FOSTER

ONCE HE STOOD ALONE BEFORE THE WALLS OF SARAMAND AND VOWED TO DESTROY IT.... AND DID.

BEFORE THE HOLY SEPULCHER IN JERUSALEM HE DEDICATED THE 'SINGING SWORD' TO THE CAUSE OF JUSTICE.

AGAIN HE MEETS ALETA, THE SMALL GOLDEN ONE, AND IS QUITE CONTENT TO LIVE UNDER HER SPELL FOREVER.

"BOSH!" EXCLAIMS WISE MERLIN, *"WITH SUCH BEAUTY AS HERS, NO SORCERY IS NECESSARY."*

PRINCE VALIANT WANDERS THE WIDE TURBULENT WORLD IN SEARCH OF ADVENTURE BUT EVER HE RETURNS TO SEE IF HER SPELL STILL HOLDS, AND IS GLAD IT DOES.

PAGE **2000**   6-8   NEXT WEEK – *Page Two Thousand and One*

Our Story: THE HALLS OF CAMELOT RING WITH MUSIC AND LAUGHTER IN CELEBRATION OF THE WINTER SOLSTICE. FROM NOW ON EACH DAY WILL BECOME LONGER.

PRINCE VALIANT MINGLES WITH THE GAY THRONG AND WITH GLIB TONGUE AND READY WIT ADDS TO THE MERRIMENT.

BUT OFTEN HE STEALS AWAY TO DREAM OF ALETA IN FAR-OFF THULE. DOES SHE KNOW WHERE HE IS? OR EVEN IF HE HAS SURVIVED THE BATTLE OF THESSALRIGA?

KING AGUAR IS CONTENT. THE NOISY ACTIVITY OF HIS GRANDCHILDREN AND THE SERENE COMPETENCE OF ALETA FILL THE CASTLE WITH HAPPINESS. BUT, ALAS, A HAPPINESS ALL TOO BRIEF.

FOR QUEEN ALETA, BY HER OWN DECREE, MUST RETURN TO THE MISTY ISLES EVERY THREE YEARS, AND THREE YEARS HAVE PASSED.
SHE ORDERS HER SLEIGH AND TRAILBREAKERS, AND BEGINS A WINTER JOURNEY.

A JOURNEY THAT ENDS AT THE SHIPYARD OF GUNDAR HARL. WHERE, TO HER SURPRISE, A READY WELCOME AWAITS HER ARRIVAL. "WE WERE EXPECTING YOU," SAYS GUNDAR, "FOR THE THREE YEARS OF ABSENCE FROM YOUR KINGDOM IS NEAR.

2001

"ALL WINTER I HAVE WORKED ON MY SHIP TO MAKE IT FIT TO CARRY A QUEEN AND HER ROYAL FAMILY.
"WE NEED FEAR NO PIRATE FOR THEY HAVE ALL FOLLOWED BELLA GROSSI TO THEIR DOOM. BUT THEY RAVAGED THE COAST AND FAMINE WILL MENACE OUR JOURNEY TO THE MISTY ISLES."

NEXT NEXT- The Premature Journey

6-5

Our Story: IN FARAWAY THULE SPRING IS STILL TWO MONTHS AWAY, BUT QUEEN ALETA IS ALREADY PREPARING FOR HER RETURN TO THE MISTY ISLES.

IN CAMELOT THERE IS MUSIC AND GAIETY... AND PEACE IN THE LAND WITH NO ROBUST ADVENTURES TO LOOK FORWARD TO. PRINCE VALIANT IS BORED.

HE DREAMS CONSTANTLY OF ALETA AND HIS CHILDREN. THEN THE GALLANT SIR GAWAIN ARRIVES AND FOR A WHILE HIS LONELINESS IS PUT TO FLIGHT.

THERE IS A TOUCH OF GRAY IN GAWAIN'S GLOSSY CURLS AND THE KNIGHTS VAL KNEW WHEN HE BECAME ONE OF THE FELLOWSHIP OF THE ROUND TABLE ARE NOW BATTLE-SCARRED VETERANS. *"AM I GROWING OLD?"* HE WONDERS, FORGETTING HE WAS NOT YET EIGHTEEN WHEN HE JOINED THE FELLOWSHIP.

THERE COMES A SPELL OF SUNNY WEATHER. THE SNOW MELTS, THE ROADS DRY OUT, AND VAL—GIVING WAY TO HIS IMPATIENCE—MOUNTS AND RIDES FORTH.

BUT THE WEATHER CHANGES AND AS HE SEEKS SHELTER HE GRUMBLES: *"ONLY AN IDIOT WOULD TRAVEL AT THIS TIME OF YEAR. OH, WHY DID I LEAVE CAMELOT!"* 2002

HE SOUNDS A BLAST ON THE HORN THAT HANGS ON A CHAIN AND THE GATES SWING OPEN AND HE IS WELCOMED IN, BUT AT A PRICE...

... THE VILLA IS FILLED WITH A PUNGENT STENCH THAT HAS EVERYONE SNIFFLING AND WIPING THEIR EYES. HIS HOST COUGHS A GREETING, THEN TURNING, WHEEZES: *"BRING OUT THAT CONFOUNDED WIZARD, HIS MEDICINES ARE WORSE THAN OUR AILMENTS."*

NEXT WEEK- *The Charlatan* 6-22

Our Story: PRINCE VALIANT WONDERS IF HE MADE A MISTAKE IN SEEKING SHELTER HERE, FOR THE VILLA IS FILLED WITH A HORRIBLE STENCH THAT HAS EVERYONE HOLDING THEIR NOSE.
AFTER A HASTY GREETING THE HOST BELLOWS: *"BRING FORTH THAT IMPOSTOR WHO CALLS HIMSELF A PHYSICIAN!"*

THERE IS SOMETHING FAMILIAR ABOUT THE ABSURD LITTLE FIGURE THAT ENTERS, EXCLAIMING: *"OPEN THE WINDOW, REMOVE THE FUME POTS AND PUT AWAY YOUR HANDKERCHIEFS. FOR I, OOM-FOOYAT, HAVE FOUND A CURE FOR THE COMMON COLD!"*

THEN HE GIVES A SHOUT OF JOY: *"VAL, MY PRINCE, MY FRIEND! HOW GLAD I AM TO SEE YOU AGAIN!"* AND TEARS OF GLADNESS SHINE IN HIS EYES.

WHEN THE ROOM IS AIRED, MANY WHO HAVE HEAD COLDS FIND THEY CAN BREATHE AGAIN. *"YOUR HELL'S-BREW IS EFFECTIVE, BUT WHAT ARE THE ODORIFEROUS INGREDIENTS?"* OOM ANSWERS: *"CAMPHOR, TURPENTINE, SULPHUR, A BIT OF TAR, SOME VINEGAR AND JUST A TOUCH OF POLECAT ESSENCE. EFFECTIVE, IS IT NOT?*

"SIR VALIANT, YOU KNEW ME AS AN INEPT WIZARD, A CHARLATAN. THEN I MARRIED WINNIE-THE-WITCH AND SHE TAUGHT ME THE HEALING ART, USING HERBS AND SIMPLES TO CURE AILMENTS. NOW I ASPIRE TO BECOME A PHYSICIAN."

WELL DOES VAL REMEMBER THAT PECULIAR WEDDING CEREMONY.

OOM FIRST REPEATS THE MARRIAGE SERVICE OF THE ANCIENT SCYTHIANS, THEN A CEREMONY PREFERRED BY THE HILL PEOPLE OF HEDONIA. TO MAKE SURE, HE ADDS AN ESPOUSING RITUAL GREATLY APPROVED IN LOWER ALCIA, THEN FORGETS THE LAST PART AND PERFORMS AN AFRICAN WEDDING DANCE FOR GOOD MEASURE..... SIGNING OFF WITH THE MATING CALL OF THE IRISH ELK. 2003

6-29

VAL RESUMES HIS LONELY JOURNEY, DISAPPOINTED THAT OOM-FOOYAT IS NOT THERE TO BID HIM FAREWELL: *'HE IS A PHYSICIAN NOW, PROBABLY OUT ON A HOUSE CALL.'*

NEXT WEEK — *Tragedy*

Prince Valiant
IN THE DAYS OF KING ARTHUR
BY HAL FOSTER

Our Story: PRINCE VALIANT RESUMES HIS JOURNEY, DISAPPOINTED THAT HIS OLD FRIEND, OOM FOOYAT, IS NOT THERE TO BID HIM FAREWELL. HE SOON LEARNS WHY.

IN A SUNNY GLADE HE FINDS THE DOCTOR-WIZARD SOUND ASLEEP. HE IS AWAKENED BY THE TOUCH OF A LANCE. *"WHAT ARE YOU DOING HERE,"* DEMANDS VAL, *"HIBERNATING?"*

"AH, NO, MY NOBLE PRINCE. WHEN I HEARD YOU WERE ON YOUR WAY TO LONDINIUM, I PLANNED TO TRAVEL UNDER YOUR PROTECTION." VAL FROWNS, FOR OOM IS ENCUMBERED WITH HIS ENTIRE STOCK OF MEDICINES.

IN THE LONELY VILLAGES THERE IS ALWAYS NEED FOR A DOCTOR AND OOM IS ALL TOO READY TO OFFER HIS SKILLS. VAL CHAFES AT THE DELAYS, WONDERING IF THEY WILL EVER REACH LONDINIUM.

ON DESCENDING A ROCKY DEFILE, VAL'S MOUNT WEDGES A HOOF BETWEEN TWO BOULDERS AND FALLS. IN ITS STRUGGLES, THE LEG IS SHATTERED BEYOND REPAIR. DRAWING 'THE SINGING SWORD' HE DOES WHAT IS REQUIRED.

TO ADD TO HIS SORROW HE IS NOW AFOOT WEIGHED DOWN BY AN IRON HELMET, COIF AND SHIRT OF MAIL, SWORD, AND SHIELD. IN SILENCE THEY PLOD WEARILY ON.

2004

ALTHOUGH THE BROOK IS ICY COLD, VAL MUST WASH HIS SHIRT TO EVICT SOME IRRITATING LITTLE SETTLERS WHO HAVE TAKEN UP THEIR ABODE THERE. THEN HE HEARS VOICES.

SEVERAL EVIL-LOOKING MEN ARE THREATENING OOM, AND OOM IS SMILING A WELCOME!

NEXT WEEK— The Fable of the Affectionate Dragon

7-6

Prince Valiant
BY HAL FOSTER

Our Story: PRINCE VALIANT COMES DRIPPING FROM HIS BATH TO FIND OOM FOOYAT BEING MENACED BY SEVERAL RUFFIANS. OOM IS ALL SMILES: "WE ARE SAVED BY THESE GENTLEMEN," HE ANNOUNCES. "THEY WILL TAKE OUR DRAGON AWAY."

"WHAT DRAGON? THERE ARE NO DRAGONS HEREABOUTS," DECLARES ONE RASCAL.
"NOT SO," ANSWERS OOM, "FOR, SEVERAL DAYS AGO, WE MET THE AFFECTIONATE DRAGON AND HAVE NOT EATEN SINCE.

"BUT LET ME TELL YOU THE STORY: ONE DAY I WAS DINING WHEN SOMETHING STUCK ITS NOSE INTO MY PLATE. I SLAPPED IT AWAY. I HEARD A SOBBING AND SNIFFLING. I LOOKED UP AND THERE WAS THE DRAGON.

"TEARS WERE RUNNING DOWN ITS CHEEKS, SO I SOOTHED HER AND GAVE HER MY DINNER. SHE HAS COME TO DINNER EVER SINCE. ONCE WE TRIED NOT TO FEED HER AND SHE ATE OUR HORSES, AS YOU CAN SEE!"

"WE ARE STARVING, FOR SHE GAMBOLS THROUGH THE VILLAGE STREETS EATING A DOG OR TWO AND MAYBE A COW, AND THE FRIGHTENED SERFS LOCK THEIR DOORS AND WILL NOT OPEN THEM TO GIVE US FOOD.

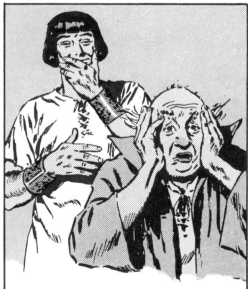

"SO WE STARVE, AND THIS VENISON YOU SEE COOKING IS NOT ENOUGH TO SATISFY HER HUNGER. WHEN WE ARE GONE SHE WILL FOLLOW YOU GENTLEMEN."

"DO YOU BELIEVE THAT DRAGON STORY?" PANTS ONE RUFFIAN. "NO," GASPS THE OTHER, "THERE ARE NO DRAGONS HEREABOUTS."

NEXT WEEK:
A Horse! A Horse!

2005

7-13

Prince Valiant
IN THE DAYS OF KING ARTHUR
BY HAL FOSTER

Our Story: PRINCE VALIANT AND OOM, FOOTSORE AND WEARY, TRUDGE THE MUDDY ROAD TO LONDINIUM.

RISING ABOVE PASTURES AND TILLED FIELDS IS A VILLAGE. "PERHAPS WE CAN BUY A MOUNT HERE TO SPEED US ON OUR JOURNEY."

BUT THIS IS A FARMING COMMUNITY, THEIRS ARE STOLID WORK HORSES. HOWEVER, THEY MUST TAKE WHAT IS OFFERED.

PRINCE VALIANT, HEIR TO THE THRONE OF THULE, KNIGHT OF THE ROUND TABLE, HERO OF MANY ADVENTURES, RUMBLES ONWARD IN A SQUEAKY CART DRAWN BY A SWAYBACKED NAG.

THEY ARE PREPARING THEIR MIDDAY MEAL WHEN A RESPLENDENT YOUNG KNIGHT DRAWS UP WITH A FLOURISH AND DISMOUNTS.

"I AM HUNGRY. I'LL BUY YOUR DINNER. HERE, VARLETS," AND HE FLINGS A FEW COINS AT THEIR FEET.

2006

QUIETLY VAL GOES BEHIND THE WAGON AND TAKES UP HIS ARMS.

"YOUNG MAN, YOU FLUNG SOME COINS IN THE MUD AND TOOK OUR DINNER. I WILL DO BUSINESS IN THE SAME WAY. HERE! I FLING A GOLD COIN IN THE MUD AT YOUR FEET AND BUY YOUR HORSE."

7-20 NEXT WEEK – *The Singing Helmet*

Our Story: *"TAKE BACK YOUR GOLD, YOU HUCKSTER. I DID NOT AGREE TO SELL MY MOUNT!"* STORMS THE ARROGANT YOUTH. PRINCE VALIANT SMILES: *"WE DID NOT AGREE TO SELL OUR DINNER FOR A HANDFUL OF PENNIES, YET YOU TOOK IT..."*

"BUT A KNIGHT, NO MATTER HOW IMPOLITE HE MAY BE, SHOULD NOT GO AFOOT, SO I THROW MY HORSE INTO THE BARGAIN."

"DRAW, SCOUNDREL, FOR NO ONE TRIFLES WITH AARON FITZOWEN!" AND HE DRAWS HIS SWORD WITH A FLOURISH.

POOR AARON, HE ALLOWS HIS TEMPER TO GUIDE HIS ATTACK AGAINST A VETERAN OF MANY DUELS.
"YOUR SWORDSMANSHIP DOES NOT JUSTIFY YOUR CONCEIT," SMILES VAL, AS, WITH THE FLAT OF HIS SWORD, HE MAKES AARON'S HELMET RING LIKE A BELL.

AARON CAN DEVISE NO DEFENSE AGAINST THE STROKES THAT COME FROM EVERY ANGLE. WEARY, STUNNED, HE SINKS TO HIS KNEES.

"I YIELD," HE MUTTERS, *"KILL ME IF YOU WILL."* HE RECEIVES NO ANSWER AND LOOKING AROUND SEES HIS OPPONENT RIDING AWAY ON HIS SPIRITED STALLION.   2007

AND SO IS JUSTICE DONE IN THE DAYS OF KING ARTHUR. AARON FITZOWEN ASTRIDE A SWAYBACKED CART HORSE RETURNS TOWARD LONDINIUM BEREFT OF CONCEIT AND ARROGANCE....... A GREAT IMPROVEMENT.

VAL AND OOM COME IN SIGHT OF LONDINIUM. THE LONG JOURNEY ACROSS BRITAIN ENDED, THE SEARCH FOR ALETA BEGINS.
NEXT WEEK— *Chivalry*
7-27

Prince Valiant
IN THE DAYS OF KING ARTHUR
BY HAL FOSTER

Our Story: AT LONG LAST PRINCE VALIANT AND OOM FOOYAT ARRIVE AT LONDINIUM. TO THE CAPTAIN OF THE GUARDS VAL SAYS: "IN A FEW DAYS YOUNG AARON FITZOWEN WILL ARRIVE. GIVE HIM THIS HORSE AND SADDLE, ALSO THIS LETTER."

WHEN AARON FINALLY COMES PLODDING IN HE FINDS HIS STEED AWAITING HIM AND A MESSAGE THAT READS: "I RETURN THE MOUNT YOU UNWILLINGLY SOLD TO ME. DISTRIBUTE THE PRICE AMONG THE POOR. MAY YOUR WISDOM INCREASE." THUS WAS CHIVALRY PRACTICED IN THE DAYS OF KING ARTHUR.

VAL FINDS HIS SHIP AND IT IS IN A MESS, FOR THE CREW HAD WINTERED ABOARD. THEY WOULD RATHER HAVE GONE BRAWLING ABOUT THE STREETS, BUT THE VESSEL CONTAINS THEIR SHARE OF THE PLUNDER WON AT THE BATTLE OF THESSALRIGA.

OOM TROTS OFF TO FIND HIS WIFE, WINNIE-THE-WITCH. IN HER LITTLE APOTHECARY SHOP WHERE SHE SELLS SIMPLES, HERBS, CATHARTICS, LOVE PHILTERS AND CHARMS, THEY MEET... TO PROVE ONCE AGAIN THAT ROMANCE IS NOT ONLY FOR THE YOUNG AND HANDSOME.

SIX MONTHS HAVE PASSED SINCE VAL LAST SAW HIS FAMILY AND HE IS ANXIOUS TO RETURN. HOPING TO PROCEED NORTHWARD BETWEEN WINTER STORMS, THE VOYAGE BEGINS.

2008

BY HER OWN DECREE, QUEEN ALETA MUST RETURN TO THE MISTY ISLES EVERY THREE YEARS.... AND THE TIME HAS COME. ONLY THE SAILING SHIP OF GUNDAR HARL DARES FACE THE WINTRY SEAS OF THULE.

NEXT WEEK— Dark Eyes Calling   8-3

Our Story: IN A SHELTERED COVE ON THE FAR NORTHERN TIP OF CALEDONIA, PRINCE VALIANT AWAITS THE END OF THE WINTER STORMS. HE AND HIS CREW ARE ANXIOUS TO SAIL HOMEWARD AND ARE WILLING TO TAKE CHANCES.

WHILE IN FAR-OFF THULE HIS FAMILY BOARDS THE SAILING SHIP OF GUNDAR HARL, AND WORK THEIR WAY SOUTHWARD, SHELTERED FROM THE WINTER GALES BY THE MANY ISLANDS.

AT BERGEN THEY WAIT THE COMING OF SPRING, THEN BEGIN THE FIVE-HUNDRED MILE CROSSING OF THE NORTH SEA. THE GODDESS OF CHANCE SMILES UPON THEM. FOR IN ALL THIS VAST EXPANSE THE TWO SHIPS MEET.

GUNDAR TURNS HIS SHIP BROADSIDE, AND IN HER LEE PRINCE VALIANT IS HOISTED ABOARD.

HOW WONDERFUL IT IS TO REST SURROUNDED BY HIS HAPPY FAMILY AFTER SO LONG AN ABSENCE. ALETA STRIVES TO PLEASE HIM, FOR WELL SHE KNOWS THAT HE WILL LONG FOR ADVENTURE AND GROW RESTLESS.

PRINCE ARN HAD ELECTED TO REMAIN IN THULE TO STUDY IN KING AGUAR'S LIBRARY, BUT WITH THE COMING OF SPRING HE DECIDES TO EXPAND THE SCOPE OF HIS LEARNING.

HE WISHES TO LEARN, FOR INSTANCE, IF THE DARK EYES OF LYDIA STILL SMILE A WELCOME, OR IF BEING A NEW-MADE PRINCESS HAS CHANGED HER.

THE LITTLE STREAMS HE HAS TO CROSS HAVE BECOME ANGRY TORRENTS FROM MELTING SNOW AND HE RIDES UP THE VALLEY SEEKING A CROSSING.

NEXT WEEK— The Wild People

2009   8-10

Prince Valiant IN THE DAYS OF KING ARTHUR
BY HAL FOSTER

Our Story: IN THE SPRING YOUNG PRINCE ARN'S FANCY TURNS TO THOUGHTS OF LYDIA, BUT THE STREAMS ARE SWOLLEN WITH MELTING SNOW. HE RIDES UP THE VALLEY IN SEARCH OF A CROSSING.

HE FINDS HIMSELF IN A CONFUSION OF MOUNTAINS AND VALLEYS. HE CHOOSES ONE THAT SEEMS TO LEAD IN THE DIRECTION HE WISHES TO GO.

ARN IS ABOUT TO TURN BACK WHEN HE COMES UPON A WIDE PLATEAU WHERE CATTLE GRAZE IN GREEN MEADOWS AND PLOWMEN TILL THE SOIL.

HE IS SURPRISED TO FIND NORSEMEN LIVING SO FAR FROM THE SEA. SUDDENLY TWO WILD-LOOKING YOUTHS SPRING FROM THEIR HIDING PLACE, WEAPONS READY, AND STARE AT HIM IN SILENCE.

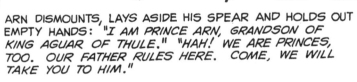

ARN DISMOUNTS, LAYS ASIDE HIS SPEAR AND HOLDS OUT EMPTY HANDS: "I AM PRINCE ARN, GRANDSON OF KING AGUAR OF THULE." "HAH! WE ARE PRINCES, TOO. OUR FATHER RULES HERE. COME, WE WILL TAKE YOU TO HIM."

THEY LEAD THE WAY, RUNNING TIRELESSLY LIKE COURSING HOUNDS, UNTIL THEY REACH A BRIDGE. THEN ONE, WITH A MOCKING LAUGH, TRIPS THE OTHER INTO THE STREAM.

HE RISES, HIS FACE LIVID WITH ANGER, A JAGGED ROCK IN HIS HAND. THE OTHER LAD DRAWS HIS KNIFE. "HOLD!" CRIES ARN, "DOES A BIT OF HORSEPLAY JUSTIFY SUCH ANGER?"

THERE WILL BE TROUBLE, MUSES ARN. THEY ARE TWINS AND HATE EACH OTHER. THEY CANNOT BOTH INHERIT THEIR FATHER'S PLACE.

NEXT WEEK—*The House of Hate*

2010   8-17

Prince **Valiant** IN THE DAYS OF KING ARTHUR

by HAL FOSTER

Our Story: THE TWIN BROTHERS, HANTZ AND FULLA, PRESENT ARN, NOT AS A GUEST, BUT A CURIOSITY. "LOOK, SIRE, WE HAVE FOUND A STRANGER. HE CLAIMS TO BE A PRINCE."

THE BATTLE-SCARRED OLD CHIEFTAIN STARES AT THE STRANGER IN SILENCE, NEITHER HOSTILE NOR FRIENDLY.

IF ARN WAS SURPRISED AT THE FATHER'S BOORISH MANNERS, HE IS EVEN MORE SURPRISED AT THE TWINS' SHOW OF BROTHERLY AFFECTION. FOR, BUT AN HOUR AGO, THEIR HATRED FOR EACH OTHER HAD BEEN CLEARLY EVIDENT.

EVEN THE THANES PRESENT SEEM TO HAVE TAKEN SIDES, HOPING THEIR CHOICE WOULD BE THE ONE TO SUCCEED THE AILING CHIEFTAIN.

PRINCE ARN WOULD RATHER LEAVE THIS FORBIDDING PLACE BUT A STORM BREAKS, LIGHTNING FLASHES AND RAIN THUNDERS ON THE ROOF.

SUDDENLY THE BUILDING SHAKES AND AN AWFUL ROAR FOLLOWS. "WHAT IS THAT?" QUERIES ARN. "A ROCK SLIDE IN THE MOUNTAINS, QUITE CLOSE, TOO," IS THE ANSWER.

"GOOD MORNING, KING ARN," CALLS HANTZ MOCKINGLY, "WILL YOUR MAJESTY COME WITH US TO VIEW THE SLIDE?"

EVEN FROM A DISTANCE THEY CAN SEE WHERE A MOUNTAINSIDE HAS FALLEN. CLOUDS OF ROCK-DUST STILL FILL THE VALLEY.

NEXT WEEK - *The Cave of Death*

2011   8-24

Prince Valiant IN THE DAYS OF KING ARTHUR
by HAL FOSTER

Our Story: PRINCE ARN AND THE TWINS, HANTZ AND FULLA, VIEW THE ROCK-SLIDE. ONE FACE OF THE MOUNTAIN HAS TUMBLED, FILLING THE VALLEY WITH DEBRIS AND GREAT CLOUDS OF DUST. ARN POINTS: "LOOK, A CAVE HAS BEEN UNCOVERED, LET US EXPLORE IT."

RUSTED ARMOR, SKULLS AND BONES. A WAR PARTY HAD BEEN TRAPPED HERE IN ANCIENT TIMES BY ONE LANDSLIDE, UNCOVERED NOW BY ANOTHER.

A JEWELED HILT GLEAMS IN THE DUST. "MINE!" SCREAMS HANTZ, "I SAW IT FIRST!" BUT FULLA PUTS HIS FOOT ON IT: "NO! MINE!" FOR A TENSE MOMENT THEY GLARE AT EACH OTHER.....

....THEN THEIR LONG HATRED EXPLODES. THEY BECOME BERSERK IN A STRUGGLE THAT CAN ONLY END WITH ONE VICTOR.

SUDDENLY THE AGE-ENCRUSTED SHEATH COMES LOOSE EXPOSING A STILL SERVICEABLE BLADE!

2012   8-31

FULLA SCREAMS AS HE SINKS SLOWLY TO THE DUST.
"I SAW IT FIRST. HE WOULD NOT LET ME HAVE IT," MUTTERS HANTZ, AS IF THAT JUSTIFIED THE DEED.

SLOWLY HIS EXPRESSION CHANGES FROM GUILT TO TRIUMPH. AT LAST HE ALONE IS HEIR TO BECOME CHIEFTAIN OF THE TRIBE.... A KING!

NEXT WEEK— The Accusation

Our Story: HANTZ ARISES, DRIPPING KNIFE IN HIS HAND, AND GLARES AT PRINCE ARN, WITNESS TO THE DEED. ARN READIES HIS SPEAR.

HE HIDES THE KNIFE INSIDE HIS SHIRT. FOR IT WAS FOR ITS POSSESSION THAT HE HAS SLAIN HIS BROTHER.

TOGETHER THEY MAKE A SLING OF FULLA'S TUNIC AND LIFT THE BODY ON A SPEAR-SHAFT.

DOWN THE JUMBLED ROCKS OF THE LANDSLIDE THEY CARRY THEIR TRAGIC BURDEN. THE DAY IS ALMOST SPENT WHEN THEY REACH THE CHIEFTAIN'S HOUSE.

"MY BELOVED BROTHER IS DEAD!" SCREAMS HANTZ. "KILLED, NAY, MURDERED, BY PRINCE ARN. I DEMAND JUSTICE!"

"NOT SO!" REPLIES ARN ANGRILY. "LOOK! THERE IS NO BLOOD ON MY GARMENTS. WE FOUND A KNIFE WITH A JEWELLED HILT, HANTZ AND FULLA FOUGHT FOR IT. HANTZ WON AND HID THE BLOODIED KNIFE INSIDE HIS SHIRT."

HANTZ STRUGGLES LIKE A MADMAN, BUT THE KNIFE IS PRODUCED. IN SHOCKED SILENCE THEY TURN TO THE OLD CHIEFTAIN......

......"BANISHED!" HE GROWLS. THEN, WITH SADNESS IN HIS VOICE: "I HAVE NO SONS."

NEXT WEEK— *The Price of Banishment* 9-7

2013

Our Story: HANTZ MURDERED HIS TWIN BROTHER, FULLA, AND NOW THE OLD CHIEFTAIN MUST PASS JUDGMENT ON HIS REMAINING SON. BANISHMENT!

IT IS A TERRIBLE SENTENCE. AS PRESCRIBED BY LAW THE CONDEMNED IS GIVEN TWELVE HOURS TO REACH THE BORDER. BITTERLY HE CURSES HIS FATHER AND THE ASSEMBLED JARLS.

TWELVE HOURS OF SAFETY, THEN IF FOUND WITHIN THE BOUNDARIES OF THE FIEF, HE CAN BE KILLED AS AN OUTLAW. HANTZ SETS OUT, RUNNING...

..... HIS FATE UNKNOWN, FOR ARN HAD MOUNTED HIS PONY AND DEPARTED. GLAD TO GET AWAY FROM THESE BRUTAL INLAND PEOPLE AND BE ONCE AGAIN WITH THE BOISTEROUS VIKINGS OF THE FJORDS.

AND ALL THIS TIME PRINCE VALIANT HAS BEEN SAILING WITH HIS FAMILY TOWARD THE MISTY ISLES TO PUT HIS WIFE'S SMALL KINGDOM IN ORDER.

AS CONTENTMENT IS A POOR INGREDIENT FOR A STORY, WE BEGIN AGAIN WHERE IT ENDS. VAL'S WINE TURNS SOUR! SO DOES HIS DISPOSITION. HE DEMANDS THAT GUNDAR HARL TURN SHOREWARD.

2014

"THE WATER IS STALE, IT WOULD POISON A GOAT AND IT MIGHT CAUSE QUEEN ALETA TO LOSE HER TEMPER!" AT THIS DIRE THREAT GUNDAR TURNS SHOREWARD.

NEXT WEEK— The Sorcerer

9-14

Prince Valiant IN THE DAYS OF KING ARTHUR BY HAL FOSTER

Our Story: GUNDAR HARL SAILS HIS SHIP FAR OUT ON THE SEA, AWAY FROM THE ROCKS AND SHOALS. HERE HE CAN SAIL SAFELY NIGHT AND DAY. NOW IN NEED OF SUPPLIES, HE TURNS SHOREWARD GUIDED BY THE SNOWCAPPED PYRENEES.

FROM A TOWER ON HIS PALACE THE GOVERNOR SEES THE SHIP APPROACHING FROM THIS STRANGE DIRECTION, FOR ALL OTHER VESSELS COME ALONG THE COAST.

AND FROM HIS CAVERN HIGH ON THE MOUNTAINSIDE, HASHIDA THE SORCERER, WATCHES AND WONDERS. DID IT COME FROM SOME STRANGE LAND BEYOND THE HORIZON?

THE GOVERNOR IS OVERJOYED TO LEARN THE VISITORS ARE THE FAMOUS WARRIOR PRINCE VALIANT AND QUEEN ALETA OF THE MISTY ISLES... THE EXCUSE HE NEEDS FOR A PUBLIC HOLIDAY... FOR LAST YEAR THE CITY HAD BEEN SACKED BY BELLA GROSSI AND HIS SAVAGE PIRATES, AND THE HARDWORKING CITIZENS NEED A HOLIDAY.

HASHIDA COMES DOWN FROM THE MOUNTAIN AND JOINS THE MERRY CROWD, INTENT ON LEARNING ANYTHING THAT HE CAN TURN TO HIS ADVANTAGE.

2015

HE WATCHES THE GLITTERING PARADE WIND ITS WAY TO THE PALACE TO THE SOUND OF TRUMPET AND CYMBAL. THEN HE SEES ALETA, POISED AND SMILING, HER FACE RADIANT WITH HAPPINESS..... AND FOR THE FIRST TIME IN HIS DOUR LIFE HIS HEART IS TOUCHED.

NEXT WEEK—The Rose 9-21

Prince Valiant
IN THE DAYS OF KING ARTHUR
BY HAL FOSTER

Our Story: ALETA SMILES HAPPILY AT THE CROWD, AND THE BEAUTY THAT HAS TROUBLED MANY A HEART AROUSES A FIERCE PASSION IN THE BREAST OF HASHIDA THE SORCERER.

HE MUST SEE HER AGAIN! BURNING WITH ARDOR HE RACES UP TO THE HEAD OF THE PROCESSION....

.....SHOULDERING HIS WAY TO THE FRONT OF THE CROWD WHERE SHE CAN SEE AND BE ATTRACTED TO HIM.

ALETA PASSES. A TOUSLED LITTLE GIRL WAVES AND EXCLAIMS: "HELLO, PRETTY LADY!" "YOU ARE PRETTY, TOO," ANSWERS ALETA, AND TOSSES HER A ROSE. BUT A WAYWARD BREEZE BLOWS IT INTO HASHIDA'S HANDS.

THE ROSE HAS EVER BEEN A LOVE TOKEN. ELATED, HE ADVANCES BOLDLY, ONLY TO BE THROWN TO THE GROUND BY ONE OF THE STERN GUARDS.

HIS DIGNITY HAS BEEN DIMINISHED, HIS PRIDE HURT. HE RETURNS TO HIS CAVERN IN THE MOUNTAINS TO DEVISE PLANS TO SECURE HIS PRIZE.

2016

THERE IN HIS GLOOMY LABORATORY HE STUDIES ANCIENT VOLUMES ON SORCERY, SCROLLS DEALING WITH THE OCCULT AND HYPNOTISM.

9-28

WHILE ALETA, UNAWARE THAT SHE HAS BEEN CHOSEN AS A SORCERER'S BRIDE, LOOKS FORWARD TO A WEEK OF GAIETY, SO WELCOME AFTER THE LONG WEEKS AT SEA.

NEXT WEEK—Underworld Images

Prince Valiant
IN THE DAYS OF KING ARTHUR
BY HAL FOSTER

Our Story: IN HIS GLOOMY CAVERN, HASHIDA THE SORCERER, HALF-CRAZED BY HIS DESIRE FOR QUEEN ALETA, MAKES HIS DEVIOUS PLANS.

HE SUMMONS ONE OF HIS YOUNG SLAVES. HE HYPNOTIZES THE LAD, AND INTO HIS BLANK MIND PLACES HIS OWN THOUGHTS AND INSTRUCTIONS.

POSING AS A PEDDLER SELLING PRETTY TRINKETS, THE SLAVE GOES AMONG THE SERVANTS SLYLY GATHERING INFORMATION; FOR THE SERVANTS KNOW ALL THAT GOES ON IN THE PALACE.

SO GREAT IS THE SORCERER'S NEED THAT HE INVOKES THE SPIRITS OF THE HALF-WORLD. SHUDDERING IN FEAR HE GOES THROUGH THE MYSTIC RITUAL AND ASKS THEIR HELP. BUT WHETHER THE APPARITIONS HE SEES ARE REAL OR IMAGINARY HE KNOWS NOT.

HE OPENS THE STRONG ROOM AND FROM THE GREAT STORE OF TREASURE BRINGS OUT RARE JEWELS, SILKS AND SATINS, FURS AND PERFUMES, AND LOADS THEM ON PACK ANIMALS.

THEN HASHIDA, THE POTENT WIZARD, DESCENDS FROM HIS MOUNTAIN ABODE CONFIDENT THAT HE CAN WIN HIS FAIR PREY.

2017

ALETA, HIS FAIR PREY, IS ENJOYING HER STAY AT THE GOVERNOR'S PALACE, FOR ALL TOO SOON THEY MUST RESUME THEIR MONOTONOUS SEA VOYAGE. THE GOVERNOR DECLARES A GENERAL HOLIDAY AND THE WHOLE CITY IS IN A FESTIVE MOOD.

NEXT WEEK—*Hashida's Triumph*

10-5

Our Story: QUEEN ALETA GOES SHOPPING FOR HOLIDAY ATTIRE, BUT THE PIRATE RAID OF LAST SUMMER HAS LEFT LITTLE OF VALUE IN THE MARKETPLACE.

THROUGH THE CITY GATES RIDES HASHIDA THE SORCERER, FOLLOWED BY A TRAIN OF BAGGAGE MULES.

HE FINDS A SHOP WHOSE SHELVES ARE EMPTY. THE MERCHANT, HELPLESS TO RESIST THE IRON WILL AND PIERCING EYES OF THE WIZARD, IS SOON HYPNOTIZED.

ALETA ARRIVES AT THE BOOTH AND CRIES OUT IN DELIGHT AT THE JEWELED ORNAMENTS AND FABRICS OF MANY COLORS. "BUT THAT IS NOT ALL," CONFIDES THE SHOPKEEPER, "THE BEST TREASURES ARE IN THE BACK ROOM."

IN THAT ROOM STANDS HASHIDA, SUAVE, SMILING, HIS BRIGHT JEWEL SWINGING RHYTHMICALLY.
"BE SEATED, MY LADY, FOR SHOPPING IS TIRING. THE HOT SUN HAS MADE YOU SLEEPY, YES, YOU ARE SLEEPY."

HE EXERTS THE FULL POWER OF HIS WILL: "SLEEP!" ALETA'S EYES ARE BLANK. SHE MAKES ONE EFFORT TO REGAIN HER COMPOSURE, BUT THE GLITTERING JEWEL DISTRACTS HER.

"THIS WINE WILL REFRESH YOU." HE FILLS TWO GOBLETS. SHE DRINKS HERS, HE PUTS HIS DOWN, UNTOUCHED.

AND SHORTLY THEREAFTER A LITTER WITH DRAWN CURTAINS MAKES ITS WAY TOWARD THE SORCERER'S MOUNTAIN STRONGHOLD.
NEXT WEEK- The Search
2018   10-12

Our Story: AT SUNSET HASHIDA REACHES HIS ABODE WITH HIS MOST PRECIOUS TREASURE... ALETA. HE SMILES AS HE DREAMS OF THE HAPPY YEARS TO COME.

THE DRUG HAS WORN OFF, BUT SHE IS STILL IN A HYPNOTIC STATE AS HE SHOWS HER HIS VAST STORE OF TREASURES THAT WILL BE HERS, ALL HERS.

HE SEATS HER UPON A THRONE AND, KNEELING BEFORE HER, TELLS HER OF HIS LOVE AND HOW HER MERRY EYES AND LAUGHING LIPS WILL MAKE HIS DIM CAVERN A HEAVEN. HER FACE SHOWS NO EXPRESSION.

HE COMMANDS HER TO SMILE, TO LAUGH, BUT THE SMILE IS A GRIMACE, LAUGHTER A CACKLE WITHOUT HUMOR. HE HAS PLACED MANY LOVELY WOMEN UNDER HIS SPELL BUT IT IS ALWAYS THE SAME. THEY LOSE ALL THEIR CHARM AND BECOME LISTLESS DUMMIES. IS THERE NO JUSTICE?

VAL IS PACING THE FLOOR, IMPATIENT AT ALETA'S LONG ABSENCE, WHEN ONE OF HER LADIES-IN-WAITING ARRIVES. "QUEEN ALETA ENTERED A MERCHANT'S SHOP AND DISAPPEARED. HOURS HAVE PASSED AND SHE HAS NOT COME OUT!"

VAL RACES TO THE SHOP TO QUESTION THE MERCHANT, BUT THE POOR FELLOW HAS BEEN EFFECTIVELY SILENCED.

2019

THE TWO GOBLETS STAND ON THE TABLE, ONE EMPTY, THE OTHER UNTOUCHED. VAL DETECTS A SLIGHT SMELL AND TASTE OF POPPIES..... DRUGGED!

THE GOVERNOR ORDERS HIS SOLDIERS INTO THE SEARCH AND AT DAWN THEY FIND A CLUE. A LITTER HAD PASSED THE GATE THAT LEADS INTO THE MOUNTAINS WHERE HASHIDA THE SORCERER HAS HIS ABODE.

NEXT WEEK— The First Failure 10-19

Prince Valiant IN THE DAYS OF KING ARTHUR
by HaL FosTer

Our Story: ALETA HAS DISAPPEARED! PRINCE VALIANT FIGHTS BACK THE PANIC AND WITH DEADLY CALM PREPARES TO FOLLOW THE ONLY CLUE TO HER WHEREABOUTS.

AT DAWN THEY REACH THE CROSSROADS. *"THAT ONE LEADS TO THE DREAD CAVERN OF HASHIDA THE SORCERER,"* SAYS THE GUIDE. *"NOT ALL OF THOSE WHO TAKE IT RETURN."*

WITHIN THE CAVERN STANDS A GRIM AND SILENT FORTRESS. A BRIDGE SPANS A RAVINE AND LEADS TO THE GATES.

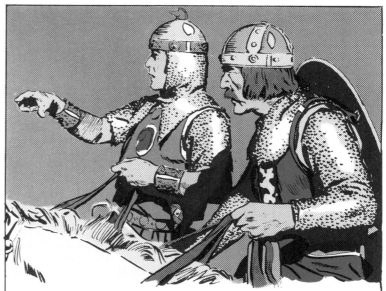

AT THE FIRST SERIES OF TALL WINDOWS VAL HESITATES TO MAKE SURE NO ARCHERS ARE WAITING. THEN, WITH A SHATTERING ROAR, HUGE BOULDERS COME POURING DOWN THE CHUTE TO CRASH ON THE ROADWAY.

"SUCH A WELCOME WOULD INDICATE OUR HOST HAS A GUILTY CONSCIENCE," OBSERVES VAL. HE FEELS SURE HIS BELOVED ALETA IS WITHIN THAT DUBIOUS CASTLE AND HE MUST FIGHT TO KEEP BACK THE PANIC THAT MIGHT LEAD TO A RASH ACTION.

FROM A TOWER WINDOW HASHIDA WATCHES THE INTRUDERS GO. HE SUSPECTS THEY CAME TO RESCUE HIS PRIZE AND LAUGHS ALOUD AT THEIR PRESUMPTION.

THEN HE GOES TO DINE IN LUXURY WITH HIS LOVELY CAPTIVE. HER BEAUTY INSPIRES HIM AS HE TELLS OF HIS GREAT LOVE AND THEIR FUTURE HAPPINESS TOGETHER. SHE HEARS NOT A WORD AND HE GAZES AT HER IN FORLORN SILENCE. *HER BEAUTY IS AS A GLITTERING JEWEL....AND JUST AS COLD.*

NEXT WEEK — *The Rope Trick*

2020

10-26

Our Story: PRINCE VALIANT FAILS IN THE FIRST ATTEMPT TO ENTER THE OMINOUS ABODE OF HASHIDA THE MAGICIAN. *"WE FAILED TO ENTER FROM BELOW, SO WE WILL TRY IT FROM ABOVE."*

IT WAS A LONG RIDE BACK TO THE CITY TO OBTAIN ROPE FOR THEIR PURPOSE, AND THE DAY IS ALMOST SPENT AS THEY BEGIN THEIR CLIMB.

IN THE GATHERING DARKNESS THEY REACH A POINT ABOVE THE CAVERN AND VAL BEGINS HIS DESCENT.

EVEN WITHOUT THE WEIGHT OF HIS ARMOR, HIS HANDS ARE CRAMPED AND BLEEDING FROM THE ROPE WHEN HE LANDS ON THE WATCHTOWER. THEN HE DRAWS THE 'SINGING SWORD.'

HASHIDA IS DESPERATE. HE HAD FIRST SEEN HER WHEN HER EYES WERE ALIGHT WITH HAPPINESS, A SMILE ON HER LIPS, AND HE HAD FALLEN IN LOVE. THROUGH TRICKERY HE HAD PUT HER UNDER A HYPNOTIC TRANCE AND NOW SHE STANDS, MUTE, UNHEEDING.

IN DESPERATION HE GRASPS HER SHOULDERS: *"LOVE ME!"* HE COMMANDS. BUT AT THE TOUCH OF HIS HANDS THE SPELL IS BROKEN. ANGER AND CONTEMPT SHINE IN HER EYES.

STILL TRYING TO DOMINATE HER, HE HOLDS ALETA CLOSE. POOR HASHIDA, NO ONE HAS EVER TOLD HIM NOT TO LAY HANDS ON A QUEEN, ESPECIALLY THIS ONE.

2021

HE YELPS WITH PAIN AS HER KEEN DAGGER SLIDES ALONG HIS RIBS. THEN HE NOTICES THEY ARE NOT ALONE. A FIGURE STANDS IN THE DOORWAY HOLDING A RESTLESS SWORD.
NEXT WEEK-A Woman's Way

11-2

Prince Valiant
IN THE DAYS OF KING ARTHUR
BY HAL FOSTER

Our Story: HASHIDA LOOKS AT THE BRIGHT BLADE, AND IN THE GRIM FACE BEYOND READS HIS DOOM. THEN ALETA CAUSES A DISTRACTION.

CONFIDENT THAT VAL'S ARRIVAL WILL SETTLE EVERYTHING, ALETA WIPES CLEAN HER SLENDER BLADE AND RETURNS IT TO HER GARTER... A GRACEFUL GESTURE THAT AWAKES HASHIDA'S DESIRE FOR HER. HE STAGGERS TO HIS FEET.

HIS HYPNOTIC EYES LOOK DEEP INTO VAL'S AS HE BEGINS HIS SOOTHING CHANT, THE DISTRACTING JEWEL SWAYING. SO! THIS IS TO BE A BATTLE OF WILLS. VAL ACCEPTS THE CHALLENGE.

HE CAN FEEL THE TERRIBLE FORCE OF THE SORCERER'S WILL AND MUST CALL ON ALL HIS STRENGTH TO HOLD HIS GAZE. "LOOK, TRICKSTER, AT THE GLEAMING GEM IN THE HILT OF THE ENCHANTED SWORD. A GEM THAT HAS WITNESSED THE DEATH OF MANY EVIL ONES. IT OUTSHINES THAT WOMAN'S BAUBLE OF YOURS!"

FOR A LONG MOMENT THEIR EYES LOCK, THEN WITH A MOAN HASHIDA CRUMPLES INTO HIS CHAIR. ALETA HOLDS OUT A RESTRAINING HAND. "PUT AWAY YOUR SWORD. YOU HAVE BROKEN HIS WILL, I HAVE STABBED HIM, AND BESIDE THAT HE LOVES ME."

"BUT, ALETA, ALL THE MORE REASON I SHOULD..." SHE INTERRUPTS HIM, "YOU CANNOT GO AROUND KILLING EVERY MAN WHO LOVES ME. YOU WOULD DECIMATE THE MALE POPULATION!"

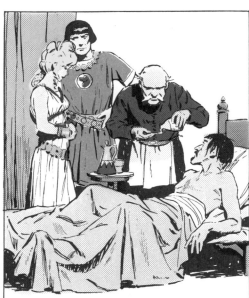

ALETA TAKES CHARGE, ORDERS THE SERVANTS TO DRESS HIS WOUND AND MAKE HIM COMFORTABLE. THEN SHE ORDERS MOUNTS TO TAKE THEM BACK TO THE CITY.

"I WISH I KNEW MORE ABOUT WOMEN," MUSES VAL. HE HAS SAID THIS CONSTANTLY SINCE HE FIRST SAW HER EIGHTEEN YEARS AGO, AND IS STILL TRYING TO FIND THE ANSWER.

2022   NEXT WEEK—Aftermath   11-9

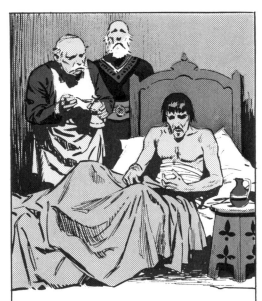

Our Story: HO-HUM, AS USUAL ALETA'S BEAUTY CAUSES A LOVELORN WIZARD TO ABDUCT HER, AND AS USUAL PRINCE VALIANT BUCKLES ON THE 'SINGING SWORD' AND RESCUES HER. OF COURSE, THE GOVERNOR IS OVERJOYED AT THE RETURN OF HIS ROYAL GUESTS. HAD AUGHT HAPPENED TO THEM HE WOULD HAVE TO FACE THE IRE OF KING ARTHUR, THE KING OF THULE AND THE NAVY OF THE MISTY ISLES.

POOR HASHIDA! HIS CHOSEN BRIDE HAD STABBED HIM; HER HUSBAND DESTROYED HIS HYPNOTIC POWER, AND WORST OF ALL CONSIDERED HIM NOT WORTHY OF KILLING!

SO THE JOLLY GOVERNOR FINDS ANOTHER EXCUSE FOR A LAVISH BANQUET. AND ALETA, FRESH AS A DAISY, IS THE LIFE OF THE PARTY... AND WHY NOT? SHE IS WELL RESTED AFTER HAVING BEEN HYPNOTIZED FOR TWO DAYS.

VAL ON THE OTHER HAND HAS NOT SLEPT FOR TWO NIGHTS. TOWARD DAWN ALETA, FOLLOWING THE SOUND OF A FAMILIAR SNORE, TRACKS HIM DOWN AND PUTS HIM TO BED.

THEIR SHIP IS PROVISIONED AND READY TO SAIL, AND THE GOVERNOR REQUESTS THEY TAKE HIS SON, HECTOR, AS FAR AS SPAIN TO CONTINUE HIS STUDIES.

2023

THE TWINS ARE DELIGHTED, FOR THEY ARE AT THAT AGE WHEN LOVE AND ROMANCE ARE ALMOST AS IMPORTANT AS FOOD...

...AND HERE, DELIVERED INTO THEIR HANDS, IS A VICTIM UPON WHOM THEY CAN PRACTICE THEIR CHARMS.
NEXT WEEK – The Sitting Duck   11-16

Our Story: THE TWIN DAUGHTERS OF PRINCE VALIANT AND QUEEN ALETA HAVE EVERYTHING THEY NEED ...EXCEPT ROMANCE. THE ONLY ONE ON THE SHIP WHO CAN SUPPLY IT IS HECTOR, A STUDENT.

VALETA UNDULATES GRACEFULLY ACROSS THE DECK, HER LASHES FLUTTERING, DIMPLES SHOWING. "OH, HECTOR, YOU ARE ALWAYS READING! IS IT ABOUT WARRIORS BOLD AND LADIES FAIR?"

"NO, I AM TRYING TO STUDY, SO IF YOU DON'T MIND....." SHE IGNORES THAT REMARK AND CONTINUES: "YOU MEN GO LAUGHING INTO DANGER WHILE WE TENDERHEARTED MAIDS CAN ONLY WAIT AND HOPE."

KAREN HAS A DIFFERENT APPROACH: "HI, HECK, PUSH OVER, I WANT TO SIT DOWN. HAS YOUR SWORD BEEN BLOODED YET?" "I HAVE NO SWORD. I AM A STUDENT," HE ANSWERS. "THEN GET ONE, FOR HOW ELSE CAN YOU PROVE YOUR WORTH EXCEPT IN BATTLE!"

DESPITE THE RISING WIND KAREN TAKES OFF HER HAIR RIBBON. "HERE, HECTOR, IS MY GAGE. WEAR IT ON YOUR SWORD ARM IN BATTLE." "HOW ROMANTIC!" SIGHS VALETA. "AND WE WILL TEND YOUR WOUNDS WHEN YOU RETURN."

"I AM NOT A WARRIOR, BUT A STUDENT!" HE DECLARES ANGRILY. "YOU GIRLS MAKE ME SICK!" HIS WORDS ARE PROPHETIC FOR JUST THEN THE SHIP HEAVES AND SO DOES HECTOR.

"HECTOR IS POOR MATERIAL FOR ROMANCE," GRUMBLES KAREN. "HE DOES NOT HAVE THE SOUL OF A POET," ADMITS VALETA.

THEY PUT HIM IN HIS BUNK. NEVER HAVING BEEN SEASICK THEMSELVES, THEY DIAGNOSE HIS ILLNESS THUS: "HE IS LOVESICK, OUR BEAUTY HAS BEEN TOO MUCH FOR HIM."
NEXT WEEK—*Duke Julian* 11-23

2024

Prince Valiant IN THE DAYS OF KING ARTHUR
By Hal Foster

Our Story: AFTER A LONG ABSENCE, QUEEN ALETA IS RETURNING TO THE MISTY ISLES TO PUT HER SMALL KINGDOM IN ORDER. HECTOR IS PUT TO WORK AS HER SECRETARY. THIS TAKES HIS MIND OFF THE TOSSING OF THE SHIP, AND ALSO KEEPS THE TWINS AT BAY.

GUNDAR CONSULTS THE STARS AND TURNS HIS SHIP EASTWARD, AND SOON THE COAST OF SPAIN COMES INTO VIEW.

ENTERING THE NEAREST PORT, THEY PAY THEIR HARBOR DUES AND STATE THEIR BUSINESS. A BERTH IS ASSIGNED THEM AT THE QUAY AND THEN THE HARBOR MASTER HURRIES AWAY, FOR HE HAS GOOD NEWS FOR HIS MASTER, DUKE JULIAN.

NOT LONG AGO THIS PORT CARRIED ON A PROFITABLE TRADE WITH THE MISTY ISLES, BUT THE DUKE HAD BEEN OVERLY AVARICIOUS AND TRADE HAD CEASED. NOW HE SEES A CHANCE TO DELUDE ITS QUEEN INTO RENEWING THAT TRADE.

VAL AND ALETA ARE SURPRISED WHEN A DELEGATION OF NOBLES BRINGS AN INVITATION FROM THE DUKE TO SPEND THEIR STAY AT THE PALACE.

THE DUKE HIMSELF CONDUCTS THEM TO HIS PALACE TO THE SOUND OF DRUMS, CYMBALS AND MARCHING FEET. BUT ONE SOUND IS MISSING: THE SHOUTS OF THE CROWD THAT USUALLY ATTEND SO FINE A PARADE. DOWN THE SIDE STREETS PEOPLE STAND IN SILENCE WHILE OTHERS PEEK FROM SHUTTERED WINDOWS. WHY?

2025

NEXT WEEK—*The Duke's Gardens* 11-30

Our Story: DUKE JULIAN LEADS THE WAY TO HIS PALACE. ON ONE SIDE OF THE ROAD RISE THE WALLS THAT ENCLOSE HIS GARDENS, WHILE ON THE OTHER, THE CROWDED HOVELS OF THE SERFS.

JULIAN TURNS TO ALETA: "I AM A GREAT ADMIRER OF BEAUTY, AS YOU WILL SEE WHEN YOU BEHOLD THE GARDENS I HAVE MADE OF THIS DESOLATE LAND."

HE SPOKE THE TRUTH, FOR THE SPLENDOR OF HIS PALACE RIVALS THOSE OF THE ANCIENT DESPOTS OF ROME.

FROM A BALCONY THEY VIEW HIS MAGNIFICENT GARDENS. WAVING HIS ARM IN A SWEEPING GESTURE HE DECLAIMS: "WOULD YOU BELIEVE THAT ONLY TEN YEARS AGO A STINKING SLUM COVERED THOSE HILLS? BUT I CLEARED AWAY THE HOVELS AND CREATED A THING OF BEAUTY!"

"WHAT BECAME OF THE PEOPLE WHO ONCE LIVED THERE?" ASKS VAL.
"I DON'T KNOW, BUT SERFS ALWAYS SEEM TO FIND A WAY TO SURVIVE SOMEHOW," ANSWERS THE DUKE.

AT DINNER THE DUKE BECOMES EXPANSIVE: "AS YOU CAN SEE, I LIVE IN THE MANNER OF THE ROMAN NOBLES WHEN ROME RULED THE WORLD AND HER CONQUERING ARMIES BROUGHT BACK TREASURE AND SLAVES. I WILL MAINTAIN THAT TRADITION UNTIL THE TIME ROME RETURNS TO POWER."

2026

"DUKE JULIAN DOES NOT SEEM TO KNOW," VAL SAYS, "THAT IT WAS THE LUXURY IN WHICH THE NOBLES LIVED THAT BROUGHT ABOUT ROME'S DOWNFALL."

12-7 NEXT WEEK— The Thin Edge

Our Story: AFTER SO MANY DAYS SPENT AT SEA, PRINCE VALIANT AND HIS FAMILY FIND IT PLEASANT TO RELAX IN DUKE JULIAN'S BEAUTIFUL GARDENS. BUT THERE ARE OTHER THINGS HAPPENING THAT ARE NOT SO PLEASANT.

AT EVENING THE OVERSEERS ROUND UP THE WORKERS AND DRIVE THEM INTO THE SLAVE COMPOUND WITH WHIPS.

DANCING GIRLS, MUSICIANS, JUGGLERS AND JESTERS ENTERTAIN AT A LAVISH DINNER. VAL AND ALETA ARE USED TO THE BRUTALITY OF MEDIEVAL TIMES, BUT THE NEEDLESS CRUELTY TO THE SLAVES SPOILS THEIR ENJOYMENT.

THE DUKE NEVER TIRES OF SHOWING HIS MAGNIFICENT GARDENS, BUT TODAY THERE IS AN ADDED ATTRACTION. BEYOND THE WALLS A COLUMN OF SMOKE BILLOWS UP FROM THE TOWN.

"ARE YOU GOING TO SEND YOUR SOLDIERS OUT TO HELP THE PEOPLE PUT IT OUT?" ASKS VAL.
"NO," ANSWERS THE DUKE, "IT'S THEIR HOUSES, LET THEM EXTINGUISH IT!"

BY NIGHTFALL THE FIRE IS OUT OF CONTROL AND EVEN FROM THAT DISTANCE THEY CAN HEAR THE OMINOUS ROAR OF THE CROWD.

THE DOWNTRODDEN PEOPLE WERE TURNING DESPERATE, VENGEFUL EYES TOWARD THE MARBLE PALACE OF THEIR OPPRESSOR.

NEXT WEEK— Terror!

2027   12-14

Prince Valiant
IN THE DAYS OF KING ARTHUR
BY HAL FOSTER

Our Story: AT THE QUAY WHERE HIS SHIP IS BEING PROVISIONED, GUNDAR HARL WATCHES THE FIRE SPREAD THROUGH THE CITY. THEN THE DOCK WORKERS DROP THEIR WORK AND RUSH UP INTO THE DOOMED TOWN.

"HECTOR, GO UP TO THE PALACE AND WARN PRINCE VALIANT THAT HE MUST RETURN TO THE SHIP WHILE THERE IS STILL TIME!"

THEN HE HAS THE ANCHOR TAKEN FAR OUT IN THE HARBOR SO THAT IN CASE OF DANGER THE SHIP CAN BE DRAWN AWAY FROM THE DOCK.

HECTOR IS RECOGNIZED BY THE PALACE GUARDS AND ALLOWED INTO THE PALACE. VAL HAS ALREADY GATHERED HIS FAMILY AND IS SEEKING A SAFE WAY OUT.

WITH THEIR HOMES AND ALL THEIR WORLDLY POSSESSIONS GOING UP IN FLAMES, THE MADDENED SERFS STORM THE PALACE. ARMED ONLY WITH CLUBS AND STONES, THEY ARE BEING SLAUGHTERED BY THE GUARDS UNTIL BY SHEER WEIGHT OF NUMBERS THEY GAIN ENTRANCE.

DUKE JULIAN HAS BROUGHT ABOUT HIS OWN DOOM. THE WALLS OF HIS GARDENS ARE SO EXTENSIVE, IT WOULD TAKE A BIGGER ARMY THAN HIS TO DEFEND THEM.

ALL ALONG THE WALLS CRAZED SERFS ARE SWARMING OVER TO INDULGE IN AN ORGY OF DESTRUCTION.

VAL CANNOT TAKE HIS FAMILY TO SAFETY BY THIS GALLERY, FOR THE MOB IS ENTERING AT THE OTHER END.

NEXT WEEK—Help from the Gods.

2028   12-21

Prince Valiant IN THE DAYS OF KING ARTHUR

BY HAL FOSTER

Our Story: AT THE FAR END OF THE 'GALLERY OF THE GODS' THE MOB IS ENTERING, BENT ONLY ON DESTROYING ALL THAT REMINDS THEM OF THEIR YEARS OF GRINDING POVERTY.

IN AN ALCOVE STANDS A BEJEWELLED STATUE OF VENUS, AND HERE PRINCE VALIANT TAKES HIS STAND. AND HECTOR, WHO HAS NEVER HELD A WEAPON BEFORE, FLOURISHES HIS HALBERD AT THE ADVANCING SERFS.

NO ONE WANTS TO BE THE FIRST TO ATTACK THE RESOLUTE WARRIOR WITH THE GLEAMING SWORD, BUT HECTOR, SWINGING HIS WEAPON WILDLY, CATCHES A PRONG IN A FOLD OF THE STATUE'S GARMENT.

PANIC LENDS STRENGTH TO HIS STRUGGLE TO FREE IT, AND THE MARBLE IMAGE COMES CRASHING DOWN, SCATTERING GEMS AND GOLDEN ALTARPIECES ACROSS THE FLOOR.

"JEWELS, GOLD, RICHES FOR THE GATHERING!" SHOUTS VAL, AND HIS WORDS CHANGE THE WHOLE DIRECTION OF THE RIOTERS' COURSE.

"LOOT NOW, DESTROY LATER!" THEY CRY AS THEY SCRAMBLE FOR THE BRIGHT ORNAMENTS. VAL LEADS HIS FAMILY AWAY. 2029

THEY REACH THE GARDENS AND ONLY THE GARDEN WALLS STAND IN THE WAY TO FREEDOM.

NEXT WEEK— *The Wallflower* 12-28

Our Story: PRINCE VALIANT LEADS HIS FAMILY OUT OF THE PILLAGED MANSION INTO THE GARDENS. FLAMES FROM THE BURNING CITY ENGULF THE MAIN GATES.

FARTHER ALONG THE WALL A FLIGHT OF STEPS LEADS TO THE TOP OF THE WALL. THE ROAR OF THE MOB DRAWS NEARER. IT IS TIME FOR DESPERATE MEASURES.

A TALL EVERGREEN OFFERS AN ESCAPE. WITH THE AID OF HECTOR'S SPEAR IT IS PULLED TOWARD THE WALL. "ALETA, YOU GO FIRST," VAL ORDERS.

"WHAT ARE YOU DOING, MY DEAR? HOW IMMODEST."
"HAVE YOU EVER TRIED TO CLIMB A TREE IN A SKIRT?" SNAPS ALETA, "AND TAKE THAT LOOK OFF YOUR FACE... LECHER!" THEN SHE DISAPPEARS INTO THE FOLIAGE.

NEXT THE TWINS. WITH SUPERB DISREGARD FOR THE OPINIONS OF MRS. GRUNDY, THEY TOSS THEIR DRESSES OVER THE WALL AND DOWN THE ESCAPE ROUTE THEY GO. HECTOR, THE STUDENT WHO HAD NEVER GIVEN A THOUGHT TO THE OPPOSITE SEX, SUDDENLY MATURES.

NOW IT IS GALAN'S TURN. HIS FATHER PICKS HIM UP AND HURLS HIM FAR OUT TOWARD THE DEEPEST PART OF THE POND WHERE HIS MOTHER WAITS TO PULL HIM ASHORE. LOTS OF FUN, REALLY.

IT HAD TAKEN THE WEIGHT OF BOTH TO HOLD THE TREE CLOSE, AND WHEN HECTOR TAKES HIS TURN VAL CANNOT MAINTAIN A HOLD AND IS LEFT ON THE WALL WITH THE TREE OUT OF REACH.

2030

"I'LL SIT HERE UNTIL THE TREE GROWS BIGGER," SAYS VAL TO HIS FAMILY BELOW. "BUT IF YOU THINK OF ANYTHING BETTER, LET ME KNOW."
NEXT WEEK—The Unhappy Landing   1-4

Prince Valiant
IN THE DAYS OF KING ARTHUR
BY HAL FOSTER

Our Story: PRINCE VALIANT STANDS ON THE WALL, HIS FAMILY SAFELY BELOW, BUT THE TREE DOWN WHICH THEY HAD ESCAPED IS NOW OUT OF HIS REACH.

THEN SOMETHING HAPPENS THAT CALLS FOR DESPERATE MEASURES. HE TAKES OFF HIS CUMBERSOME ARMOR AND TOSSES IT OVER THE WALL...

... FOR THE MOB, HAVING LOOTED THE DUKE'S MANSION, IS LOOKING FOR A WAY TO ESCAPE FROM THE GARDEN. FOR THE MAIN GATE IS BLOCKED BY THE FLAMES OF THE BURNING CITY.

VAL IS SO USED TO THE WEIGHT OF HIS ARMOR THAT HE MISJUDGES THE DISTANCE OF HIS LEAP AND LANDS NEAR THE TOP OF THE EVERGREEN...

...WHICH, BENDING UNDER HIS WEIGHT, SWAYS OUT OVER THE POND AND BREAKS.

AS ALETA SAID AFTERWARD: "MY HUSBAND DOES EVERYTHING WITH A FLOURISH. NEVER HAVE I SEEN A BIGGER SPLASH!"

2031

THE ONCE ELEGANT PRINCE ARISES, AND HIS FIRST WORDS ARE: "THE FIRST ONE WHO LAUGHS WILL BE TOSSED IN THE POND!"

ONCE MORE ENCASED IN HIS FAMILIAR HARDWARE, VAL LEADS HIS FAMILY TOWARD THE HARBOR AND THE SAFETY OF THE SHIP.

NEXT WEEK- The Slave Market

1-11

Our Story: PRINCE VALIANT LEADS HIS FAMILY DOWN FROM THE BURNING CITY AND BOARDS HIS SHIP. TO HIM IT HAD BEEN ONLY A ROUTINE EVENT.

BUT TO HECTOR THE SCHOLAR, IT HAD BEEN AN EPIC ADVENTURE: HE AND PRINCE VALIANT, SIDE BY SIDE, HAD BROUGHT THE QUEEN OF THE MISTY ISLES TO SAFETY! HE DRESSES TO SUIT THE PART.

THEY SAIL ON CADIZ WHERE HECTOR MUST LEAVE THEM TO CONTINUE HIS STUDIES. HE SALUTES VAL AS ONE HERO TO ANOTHER: "FAREWELL, SIR VALIANT, SOME DAY WE MAY SHARE ANOTHER ADVENTURE!"

FIRST THERE IS GOOD NEWS. THEY NEED FEAR NO PIRATES, FOR LAST YEAR BELLA GROSSI HAD ENLISTED THE VERY SCUM OF THE INLAND SEA ON HIS ILL-FATED BID TO BECOME TYRANT OF THE BALTIC SEA. NONE HAD RETURNED.

THEN THE BAD NEWS: ALETA IS IN REVOLT! "TOO LONG HAVE I BEEN COOPED UP ON SHIPBOARD. I NEED A HAIRDRESSER, A PERSONAL MAID! MY HAIR SMELLS LIKE SEAWEED, AND I'D LIKE A SALT HERRING!"

PRINCE VALIANT IS NOT COMPLETELY FEARLESS. "GUNDAR, PUT INTO TANGIERS, FOR I SEE A STORM APPROACHING IN MY WIFE'S EYES."
2032

AT A SLAVE MARKET IN TANGIERS, ALETA SELECTS HER ATTENDANTS. SLAVERY IS NOT ALL WHIPS AND CHAINS, FOR MANY WILLINGLY SELL THEMSELVES INTO SERVICE TO AVOID A LIFE OF POVERTY IN THE CITIES' STINKING SLUMS.

NEXT WEEK — Labor Problems

1-18

Our Story: IN A TANGIERS SLAVE MARKET ALETA PURCHASES A WARDROBE MISTRESS, A HAIRDRESSER AND A HANDMAIDEN. THEY ARE QUITE EXPENSIVE.

THEN THEY HAVE TO BE DRESSED AS BEFITS THE ATTENDANTS OF A QUEEN. AND THE QUEEN, TOO, FINDS MANY THINGS IN THE BAZAAR SHE FANCIES. FOUR WOMEN ON A SHOPPING SPREE WITH AN UNLIMITED EXPENSE ACCOUNT!

AT DAY'S END A TIRED BUT HAPPY ALETA AND HER SLAVES RETURN TO THE SHIP WITH THEIR PURCHASES... AND THE BILL.

CAPTAIN GUNDAR WATCHES THE NEW ADDITIONS TO THE PASSENGER LIST COME ABOARD:
"I SHOULD HAVE BUILT A LARGER SHIP," HE COMPLAINS. AND AS VAL PAYS THE MERCHANTS, HE MUTTERS:
"ONE MORE SHOPPING TOUR LIKE THIS AND WE WILL HAVE TO TURN TO PIRACY TO PAY THE BILLS!"

QUEEN ALETA HAD PURCHASED EVERY LUXURY SHE COULD THINK OF, SAVE ONE. ON HER WAY TO THE MISTY ISLES TO RESUME HER THRONE THERE ARE PROCLAMATIONS, SPEECHES AND NEW LAWS TO WRITE. A GREAT VOLUME OF WRITING TO DO.... AND SHE HAS NO SECRETARY.

A YOUNG MAN COMES ABOARD. HE HAS A LOOK OF QUALITY BUT WEARS A SLAVE COLLAR.
"BUY ME, SIRE, I HAVE A SECRET THAT WILL ENRICH WHOEVER SETS ME FREE."

2033 NEXT WEEK– The Usurer 1-25

Prince Valiant
IN THE DAYS OF KING ARTHUR
BY HAL FOSTER

Our Story: "TO GET THE SHIP I NEEDED TO SEARCH FOR THE TREASURE, I BORROWED MONEY FROM A BANKER. BUT BEFORE WE COULD SAIL, HE CALLED IN THE LOAN AND SEIZED THE SHIP."

"HE CLAIMS I SIGNED A CONTRACT BY WHICH I MUST WORK AS HIS SECRETARY UNTIL THE DEBT IS DISCHARGED."

QUEEN ALETA SITS AMID A MASS OF DOCUMENTS THAT MUST BE PUT IN ORDER BEFORE SHE RESUMES HER THRONE. AT THE WORD 'SECRETARY' SHE LEAPS TO HER FEET......

....."BUY HIM FOR ME, VAL. I DESPERATELY NEED A SECRETARY. BETTER STILL, LET US VISIT THIS BANKER WHO CLAIMS TO HOLD SUCH AN UNFAIR CONTRACT."

"THE CONTRACT IS HERE, ALL SIGNED AND LEGAL," SNEERS THE BANKER.
"BUT HIS SHIP," ASKS VAL, "WHERE IS IT?"
"OH, I SOLD IT TO MEET EXPENSES."
"THEN YOU GOT YOUR MONEY BACK AND THE LAD'S DEBT IS DISCHARGED," ANNOUNCES ALETA.

"AH! BUT BY THE RULES OF THIS CONTRACT..." BEGINS THE MONEY LENDER. BUT VAL IS TIRED OF ALL THIS TALK. HE GATHERS UP THE CONTRACT AND THE BANKER.
"LET THE CHIEF MAGISTRATE RULE ON THIS AND YOUR RIGHT TO PUT A SLAVE COLLAR ON A FREE MAN."

THE PAIN OF A MAN WHO HAS DISTURBED A WASPS' NEST IS AS NOTHING COMPARED TO THE AGONY OF A USURER WHO HAS LOST A PROFIT. TO EASE HIS MISERY VAL TOSSES HIM HIS PURSE. 2034

HE BITES EACH COIN TO MAKE SURE IT IS GENUINE BEFORE SAYING THANKS, AND ZILLA BECOMES ALETA'S SECRETARY.
NEXT WEEK- *Love's Labor Lost* 2-1

Prince Valiant
IN THE DAYS OF KING ARTHUR
BY HAL FOSTER

Our Story: GUNDAR HARL LOOKS AT ALETA'S GAILY-COLORED RETINUE AND GRUMBLES: "EACH DAY MY SHIP OF WAR LOOKS MORE AND MORE LIKE CLEOPATRA'S BARGE."

ALETA PUTS DOWN HER WORK. "WHERE IS VAL? HE HAS NOT MADE LOVE TO ME FOR DAYS. I HAVE NEGLECTED THE DEAR BOY AND MUST MAKE AMENDS."

HER THREE HANDMAIDENS GO TO WORK WITH A WILL, FOR THIS IS THEIR FIRST OPPORTUNITY TO DEMONSTRATE THEIR CRAFT.

VAL AND GUNDAR WATCH AN APPROACHING SQUALL. ORDERS ARE GIVEN TO SHORTEN SAIL AND PREPARE FOR A BLOW. "IT WILL NOT LAST LONG BUT IT WILL BE VIOLENT," GUNDAR OBSERVES.

DRESSED IN ONE OF HER NEW GOWNS, ALETA PREPARES TO REKINDLE THAT LOOK IN VAL'S EYES.

ALETA AND THE SQUALL REACH THE DECK AT THE SAME TIME. THE DOOR SLAMS SHUT.

VAL APPEARS OUT OF THE MIST: "OH, HELLO, DEAR. WHAT ARE YOU DOING OUT IN THE RAIN?" HE ASKS CHEERFULLY, "WON'T YOU GET WET?"

"SO THE WIND BLEW THE DOOR SHUT," LAUGHS VAL. "OH, THAT WAS FUNNY!"
"AND A HA-HA TO YOU," SNAPS ALETA. "WHEN I RESUME THE THRONE, I'LL MAKE YOU CHIEF JESTER, FUNNYMAN!"

2035 NEXT WEEK - Bittersweet   2-8